THE OFFICIAL
RANGERS
ANNUAL

2002

Written by
Douglas Russell

g

A Grange Publication

© 2001. Published by Grange Communications Ltd., Edinburgh, under licence from Rangers Football Club. Printed in the EU.

ISBN 1-902704-11-8

THE MEMBERS' CLUB AT IBROX

Contents

JIM BAXTER

THE BLUE BRAZILIAN

JIM BAXTER

Touched by genius and, maybe just, the most naturally gifted Ranger of them all, James Curran Baxter arrived at Ibrox in the summer of 1960 following the payment of a then £17,500 Scottish record fee to Raith Rovers.

The signing of this immense talent was, in many ways, the completion of a jigsaw and manager Scot Symon's good team would soon be considered great. The orchestra had found its conductor and midfielder 'Slim Jim' became the creative, controlling force of a Rangers squad that would dominate Scottish Football for some four to five years. Even today, that side of the early sixties (which included the likes of Jimmy Millar, Ralph Brand and Davie Wilson) is still considered one of the greatest in the club's long and illustrious history.

Celtic were waiting at Parkhead in only the second league game of Season 1960/61. By crushing them 5-1, Rangers recorded one of their most impressive victories in the east end of Glasgow and set off full of confidence on the road to championship glory. Although there was no league title the following year, both the Scottish and League Cups ended up on display in the Ibrox Trophy Room. Season 1962/63 witnessed a Championship and Scottish Cup 'double' with a glorious 'treble' in place by the following year and Celtic beaten no less than five times in five meetings. During the period 1960-65, Jim Baxter wore the blue of Rangers against Celtic on a total of eighteen occasions, tasting the bitterness of defeat only twice.

Worshipped for both his supreme left foot (he called it 'The Glove') and his ability to 'partake the Michael' on the football field, Jim truly excelled in the heat of the 'Old Firm' infernos. This was his stage. The Scottish Cup Final of 1963 (the first involving the clubs for thirty-five years) was a case in point.

After a 1-1 draw in the first game, a crowd of some 120,000 gathered for the replay. Still recalled as one of the most one-sided finals ever, Rangers turned on the style as the 'follow-follow' brigade turned up the volume. With tormentor-in-chief 'Slim' orchestrating from midfield, the 3-0 scoreline hardly conveyed blue superiority on the day. Indeed with some twenty minutes (!) still remaining, the green and white fans deserted the Hampden slopes en masse and left for an early fish supper, having seen and suffered enough. Celtic had merely been the audience to a Baxter master-class, although little applause was forthcoming at the end of the lesson.

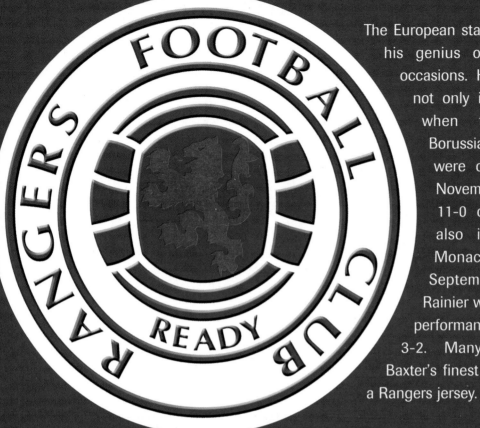

The European stage was also privy to his genius on several glorious occasions. He was outstanding not only in the rain of Ibrox when the Germans of Borussia Monchengladbach were crushed 8-0 in late November 1960 (aggregate 11-0 over two legs!) but also in the warmth of Monaco the following September when Prince Rainier was treated to a royal performance as Rangers won 3-2. Many considered this Baxter's finest European display in a Rangers jersey.

In the dark blue of Scotland, he was just as much a revelation, with two games in particular, both against England, standing out. At Wembley in 1963, he not only tormented the life out of those white shirts but also netted both his country's goals (one a penalty despite the fact that he had never taken a spot-kick before!) in a 2-1 win. Four years later, it was even more satisfying, when the recently crowned World Champions were beaten 3-2, with Baxter again reigning supreme at the Wembley carnival and scoring twice into the bargain. The player earned 34 Scotland 'Caps' in total.

After initial success in Season 1964/65 (Jim captained Rangers to a 2-1 League Cup Final victory over Celtic), tragedy struck further afield in Europe when, very late on in the game with Rapid Vienna in early December, he suffered a leg break. Baxter had been quite magnificent that day in the intimidating atmosphere of the Prater stadium, leading his side to a 2-0 victory in the Austrian capital as Rangers progressed to the last eight of the European Cup on a 3-0 aggregate score.

In May 1965, the player joined Sunderland before moving to Nottingham Forest (for £100,000) some two and a half years later. Jim Baxter returned to his first love Rangers in May of 1969 (on a free transfer) before retiring from the game aged just thirty. He had played 254 games and scored 24 goals for the Ibrox club, winning three League Championships as well as three Scottish and four League Cup medals along the way.

Jim Baxter died of cancer on April 14, 2001. The phrase 'we will never see his like again' has seldom sounded so true. The 'Blue Brazilian'- he was, quite simply, the best.

RANGERS IN EUROPE QUIZ

1. In what years did Rangers reach the final of the European Cup Winners' Cup?

2. Giovanni van Bronckhorst scored in three consecutive Champions' League games last season. True or false.

3. What happened when Rangers entertained East German Champions Vorwarts in the European Cup of Season 1961/62?

4. Name the scorers at Elland Road when Leeds were beaten in the European Cup, November 1992.

5. Rangers have knocked Juventus out of the European Cup. True or false.

6. What was the score when the 'Light Blues' travelled to the Soviet Republic to play the Russian champions Vladikavkaz in the European cup of Season 1996/97?

7. Who did Rangers meet in the final of the 1967 Cup Winners' Cup?

8. The teams met again in the semi-final of the same competition five years later. What was the aggregate score?

9. Apart from Leeds and Tottenham Hotspur, name the other English Premiership outfit that Rangers have met in Europe.

10. In the year that the club lifted the Cup Winners' Cup (1972), who was top European scorer.

Answers on page 64.

FROM GLASGOW GREEN TO GOVAN

The earliest Rangers matches were played on the public pitches of Flesher's Haugh (on Glasgow Green) until a home ground was secured at Burnbank (near Kelvin Bridge) three years later in 1875. The following year saw a switch to Kinning Park, in the south side of the city, which remained the club's home until the move to the Ibrox area of Glasgow in August 1887. In those far-off days, Ibrox was still considered 'out in the country' but the club had rightly judged the westward spread of the city's growing population.

The site of Old Ibrox Park was adjacent to the current stadium but on the other side of Copland Road. Rangers finally made the short move to their present home in December 1899.

The stadium was built originally in response to the ever-increasing growth in popularity of the sport and to reflect Rangers' increasingly dominant position in Scottish Football. Central to the development of Ibrox was the construction of the Grandstand (today's Main Stand), officially opened on New Year's Day 1929, when Celtic were beaten 3-0. Designed by Archibald Leitch (also responsible for Everton's Goodison Park), it remains to this day a tribute to the vision of the Rangers directors of the late 1920s.

The 'New Ibrox' was instigated by the foresight of Willie Waddell in the wake of the Disaster in 1971 (when 66 Rangers fans lost their lives) and was given fresh impetus by modern safety legislation and the challenge of meeting the demanding standards of European competition. The Waddell dream was fulfilled largely through the highly successful Rangers Pools operation, which raised the £11 million needed to pay for the three new stands built during the 1970s and 1980s – the Copland Road Stand (officially opened in August 1979), the Broomloan Road Stand (August 1980) and the Govan Stand (December 1981). With the completion of the 'Club Deck' on top of the Main Stand in 1991, the all-seated capacity rose to more than 50,000 in what is now a totally enclosed ground with two huge Jumbotron screens (utilised for both 'home' and certain 'away' games) at its northern corners.

Now undoubtedly one of Europe's finest, the modern stadium still echoes its glorious past in the imposing red-brick facade of the vintage grandstand. Erected under the visionary guidance of William Struth, it now enjoys (as of 1980) the status of a listed building.

JAN WOUTERS
FIRST-TEAM COACH

PLAYING CAREER

1980 : FC Utrecht sign the twenty-year-old midfielder on professional forms.

1982 : Jan wears the orange of Holland for the first time.

1985 : In May of this year, he leads Utrecht to victory in the Dutch FA Cup Final before joining Ajax in November.

1986 : A second cup medal but this time with Ajax.

1987 : A quite superb season brings the player not only his third Dutch FA cup medal but also a European Cup Winners' Cup medal following the 1-0 defeat of Lokomotiv Leipzig in the Athens final.

1988 : Probably the highlight of his playing career when, as a member of the Dutch squad, he plays his part alongside the genius of Ruud Gullit as Holland lift the European Championship at EURO 88.

1990 : Plays for Holland in the ITALIA 90 World Cup Finals.

1991 : Ajax take the Championship and Jan secures his first league medal before, in November, heading for Germany and Bayern Munich in the Bundesliga.

1992 : With his country for EURO 92 in Sweden.

1993 : In December of this year, he returns to Holland, signing for PSV Eindhoven.

1994 : The USA and World Cup 94 beckon for the midfielder in this his fourth major international tournament. Dutch national coach Dick Advocaat appoints him team captain for America.

1996 : Ends his playing career after winning cap number 70 for his country and moves into coaching. Only five other Dutchmen had appeared more times in the orange of Holland.

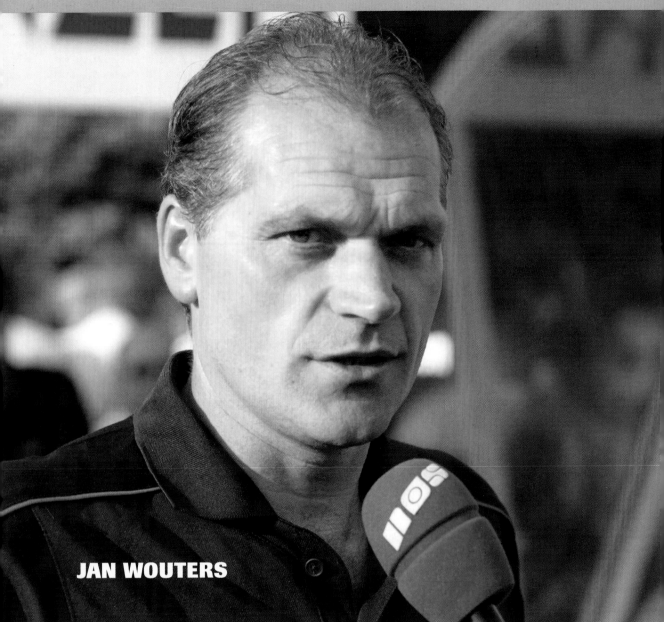

JAN WOUTERS

MANAGERIAL CAREER

1996 :   Becomes assistant manager of FC Utrecht.

1997 :   Joins Ajax as youth coach.

1998 :   Promoted to head coach at Ajax.

1999 :   First trophy in management as Ajax lift the Dutch FA Cup.

2001 :   Leaves Ajax in March before joining Rangers for the start of
         Season 2001/02.

RONALD DE BOER
IT'S A FACT!

1970 : Follows his twin-brother Frank into the world on 15 May.

1984 : The youngster joins Ajax Youth.

1987 : The seventeen-year-old makes his Ajax debut (as a substitute) in the game with PEC Zwolle.

1990 : Ajax lift the Dutch Championship.

1991 : Having played 52 games and scored 14 goals for Ajax, Ronald joins Twente Enschede. In just one-and-a-half seasons with his new club, the player nets 22 times in 49 league games and Ajax buy him back during Season 1992/93.

1993 : Appears for the first time in the orange of Holland when San Marino are beaten 6-0 in a World Cup qualifying game in Utrecht. His name was on goal number 5 that night.

1994 : Celebrates as Ajax win the championship and then plays in two games for his country in that year's World Cup Finals in the USA.

1995 : de Boer is a vital component as Ajax dominate the football headlines, winning the European Cup, the European Super Cup, the World Club Championship as well as their own domestic title in Holland.

1996 : As well as helping Ajax to another championship, Ronald plays in EURO 96 with his country.

1998 : Ajax lift the League and Cup 'double' before that year's World Cup Finals in the Netherlands. Holland reach the semi-final stage of the tournament before losing out to Brazil.

1999 : The twins join Barcelona in mid January with £15 million paid to Ajax for their joint services. Ronald had made some 296 appearances for his club (scoring 62 goals in the process) and twice been honoured with the 'Player of the Year' title in his homeland. Scores in his first game for Barcelona and ends the season as a proud owner of a prestigious Spanish Championship Medal.

2000 : Member of the Dutch squad that make it to the semi-finals of EURO 2000 and wins cap number 61. Ronald de Boer joins Rangers for approximately £4 million.

RONALD DE BOER

BLUE HEAVEN
THE IBROX TROPHY ROOM

Outstanding teams, legendary footballers and glorious occasions have all played their part in the history of Rangers. Many of these wonderful, emotional memories are brought back to life by the contents of the Ibrox Trophy Room. 15

On a visit to Spain over forty years ago, manager (and gentleman) Scot Symon witnessed at first hand the magnetic mass appeal of Real Madrid's Trophy Room and set about establishing one for his own club. Formerly the players' billiard room, it was opened in 1959 to accommodate the growing treasure trove of trophies and gifts, only some of which had previously been on display in a boardroom cabinet. Now the crowning glory of the stadium, it houses a spectacular display of silverware, porcelain, crystal and memorabilia stretching back to the very foundations of the club. Even the panelled wood on the walls is something special – it was originally intended for the great ocean liner, Queen Mary!

Like the stadium itself, the original concept of the Trophy Room has expanded but the major and most historically important elements remain in place. The oil painting of one of Britain's greatest-ever football managers William Struth (who guided the club from 1920 to 1954) still dominates the room and is surrounded by miniature replicas of many decades of League Championship flags, of which Season 1999/2000 was title number 49. Also on view are the thirty-six medals won by one of the true blue Ibrox legends (and goalscorer supreme) Bob McPhail, in addition to the Victory Cup of 1946, the Loving Cup (1937), the Bruce Casket (1941) and countless other items, each with its own tale of drama and conflict.

In 1972 the European Cup Winners' Cup famously came to rest here and the Scottish Cup has done likewise on 29 occasions – and who is to say that the old trophy, first won by Rangers in 1894, will not soon return to grace the hallowed ground. Those youthful pioneers who founded the club in 1872 could scarcely have envisaged what they had started. It took them seven years to win their first trophy (the Charity Cup) and a further twelve years to claim a second, the 'shared' Championship with Dumbarton. Of course, the old club has not done so badly since those sparse early years!

The Ibrox Trophy Room or 'Blue Heaven' . . . as more than one bluenose has commented over the years!

PICK OF THE TROPHY ROOM

THE VICTORY CUP (1946)

To celebrate the end of the Second World War, it was decided to put up a trophy for competition with the games to be played in April, May and June of 1946. As the Scottish Cup had not yet been revived, this was obviously an important and prestigious tournament.

This particular piece of silverware was originally the Scottish Emergency War Cup, which the 'Light Blues' had won at Hampden in May 1940 after beating Dundee United 1-0. Then it became the Southern League Cup (beginning with Season 1940/41) and, in six wartime competitions, was won four times by Rangers. Hibernian and Aberdeen also lifted the trophy during that period. In fact, when Aberdeen were winners in May 1946, it was the team's first-ever national trophy success. Unfortunately, the outfit from 'up north' only kept the trophy for some five weeks as the SFA asked for its return so that it could be used as the Victory Cup!

After beating Stenhousemuir, Airdrie, Falkirk and semi-final opponents Celtic (2-0 after a 0-0 draw), the Ibrox side met Hibernian at Hampden in the final on 15 June, 1946, before a crowd of nearly 100,000 spectators. With Jimmy Duncanson scoring twice and Torry Gillick netting the other, Rangers ran out impressive 3-1 victors on the day and the silverware was heading for a permanent place of honour down Govan way in the Ibrox Trophy Room.

Rangers : Brown, Cox, Shaw, Watkins, Young, Symon, Waddell, Gillick, Thornton, Duncanson and Caskie.

An interesting fact surrounds this game as it was one of the few occasions when two brothers opposed each other in a cup final at Hampden. The legendary Jock 'Tiger' Shaw was at left-back for Rangers and his brother David played in the same position for the Edinburgh side. Additionally, the pair had actually played together in the Victory International against England (1946), filling both the full-back positions in dark blue for their country. The Easter Road player was later preferred for the No.3 jersey in the national side, thus keeping Jock's tally of Scottish honours to only four.

PICK OF THE TROPHY ROOM

THE LOVING CUP (1937)

If the Trophy Room is the crowning glory of Ibrox, then The Loving Cup is the Jewel in the Crown. One of only thirty cast from a unique mould (subsequently destroyed) to commemorate the coronation of Their Majesties King George V1 and Queen Elizabeth (later Queen Mother) in May 1937, the story of how it came into Rangers' possession is part of the club's folklore.

Identical Loving Cups were presented to the 22 English First Division clubs of the time, with the remainder going to the British Museum and various other important organisations.

Then, as now, Rangers were recognised as one of the world's great clubs and so it was that they were asked to participate in a special match to raise funds for the dependants of the miners who lost their lives in the Holditch Colliery Disaster, in the Stoke area. Manager William Struth accepted the invitation without hesitation.

In appreciation, Stoke City President, Sir Francis Joseph, gifted Rangers his own club's Loving Cup after the match which had finished goalless. He requested that it should be used from then on to drink the health of the reigning monarch on the occasion of the Glasgow side's first home match of every new year. To this day, the New Year toast is celebrated in the Ibrox Blue Room by the assembled directors and guests of Rangers and their first visiting opponents.

As far as can be confirmed, the Rangers Loving Cup is one of the very few remaining and, most probably, the only one still in regular use.

19 October, 1937: Stoke City 0 Rangers 0

Rangers : Dawson, Gray, McDonald, McKillop, Simpson, Little, Main, Fiddes, Smith, Venters and Kinnear.

FIND THE LEGEND

The names of ten Rangers legends are hidden somewhere in this letter puzzle.

Can you find them?

```
C K L I U H M N B C V F S S N I K L I W
W Y O U N G U P L K J H N B V C D S T A
A S D F C V G B H T R E U P L K H N Y H
T S I O C C M R E W Q A D B N B X T R S
N T R H G K N B B A X T E R M J H K T R
A P B V G X Z A S D F G H A L J P U Y T
R T D F I J B Z G X S A E N K N B G P K
R T R D E G H B C N M K J D P T R E S R
U F R T R S A M A R O G K L O P Y T R W
D K J H G F T R E O M N V H G U O G H J
```

Answers on page 64.

PICK OF THE TROPHY ROOM

SPODE CHINA BOWL (1961)

Rangers met English Champions Wolves (who presented this exquisite gift) in the semi-final of the European Cup Winners' Cup in the spring of 1961. Although the Ibrox side had already disposed of both the impressive Hungarians Ferencvaros (5-4 aggregate) and the Germans of Borussia Monchengladbach (11-0 aggregate – yes 11-0!), Wolves were still favourites as they had won the English Championship twice in the previous three seasons and were understandably expected to go all the way to the final of this competition.

A crowd of just under 80,000 witnessed the first-leg in Glasgow. Rangers played most of the game with only ten fit men (this was in the days before substitutes were allowed) as half-back and 'iron man' Harold Davis had been injured in the first ten minutes and spent the bulk of the ninety minutes limping. However, goals from winger Alex Scott and striker Ralph Brand meant that the 'Light blues' carried a two goal advantage to Molyneux, the home ground of Wolves.

An astonishing 10,000 Rangers fans (and can you imagine the vocal support they provided!) travelled south to the snow storms of Wolverhampton in mid April for the return match. The game itself ended in a 1-1 draw after another Alex Scott special had given the lads the lead prior to the interval. 'Keeper Billy Ritchie had been superb throughout the ninety minutes but his save from a Ron Flowers thunderbolt late in the first half was nothing short of unbelievable!

Rangers had just become the first British team to reach the final of any European competition and, in doing so, helped restore a great deal of national pride to the country as Scotland had been humiliated 9-3 by England at Wembley only four days earlier.

29.3.61 :   First Leg Rangers 2 Wolves 0
Scott (33), Brand (84)

Rangers :   Ritchie, Shearer, Caldow, Davis, Paterson, Baxter, Scott, Wilson, Baillie, Brand and Hume.

19.4.61 :   Second Leg Wolves 1 Rangers 1
Scott (43)

Rangers :   Ritchie, Shearer, Caldow, Davis, Paterson, Baxter, Wilson, McMillan, Scott, Brand and Hume.

FIND THE PLAYER

Can you find the names of ten players who appeared on first team duty in Season 2000/01?

```
M D B V T O F G H J K T U G A Y R E I R
S N F R E L L I M P W E R T Y Z S A E T
W E S G H F L M I A N Y E R D G H V E I
A S D F G H J K L W O P U Y T R E C V B
R K J H M M O O R E R E U O W E R T I S
E I E R T O U P L K J H G F D C D B D M
O A E W A L L A C E P M L K J H O F N S
B E V H G S S P T Y B I M L K H D S E W
E V C E R T Y U P O W L K J H G D D S A
D R T R E W O U E R T D F G B M S O L K
```

Answers on page 64.

RANGERS

THE HONOURS

EUROPEAN CUP WINNERS' CUP

Winners 1972
Runners-up 1961, 1967

SCOTTISH LEAGUE CHAMPIONS (49)

1891, 1899, 1900, 1901, 1902, 1911, 1912, 1913, 1918, 1920,
1921, 1923, 1924, 1925, 1927, 1928, 1929, 1930, 1931, 1933,
1934, 1935, 1937, 1939, 1947, 1949, 1950, 1953, 1956, 1957,
1959, 1961, 1963, 1964, 1975, 1976, 1978, 1987, 1989, 1990,
1991, 1992, 1993, 1994, 1995, 1996, 1997, 1999, 2000.

SCOTTISH CUP WINNERS (29)

1894, 1897, 1898, 1903, 1928, 1930, 1932, 1934, 1935, 1936,
1948, 1949, 1950, 1953, 1960, 1962, 1963, 1964, 1966, 1973,
1976, 1978, 1979, 1981, 1992, 1993, 1996, 1999, 2000.

SCOTTISH LEAGUE CUP WINNERS (21)

1946/47, 1948/49, 1960/61, 1961/62, 1963/64, 1964/65,
1970/71, 1975/76, 1977/78, 1978/79, 1981/82, 1983/84,
1984/85, 1986/87, 1987/88, 1988/89, 1990/91, 1992/93,
1993/94, 1996/97, 1998/99.

Under manager Bill Struth's guidance in Season 1929/30, Rangers
achieved a unique feat, never since equalled anywhere in the world,
by winning every competition for which they were eligible to enter.

**The complete haul was: Scottish Cup, League Championship, Glasgow Cup,
Glasgow Charity Cup, Second Eleven Cup and Scottish Alliance
(Reserve League Championship).**

WILLIAM STRUTH

ON THE WING

For some forty years, beginning in the post-war era, Rangers were more than just a little fortunate when it came to the number 7 jersey. Quite simply, in each of those four decades, a quartet of true blue legends filled that right-wing position – Willie Waddell, Alex Scott, Willie Henderson and, arguably the most talented of them all, Tommy McLean.

Manager Willie Waddell brought the Kilmarnock player to Ibrox in 1971 for some £65,000. McLean was, by this time, in his mid twenties and had represented Scotland five times during his time down the coast in Ayrshire. In fact, it was Waddell who had taken the youngster to Kilmarnock when he was manager there. At Rangers, Tommy was an altogether different type of winger than his lauded predecessors, for his true skill was pin-point accuracy with a football, whether it be a cross or a pass. Both the 'Derek' centre-forwards (Johnstone and Parlane) converted chances by the barrowload that were created by him.

By the end of his first season with Rangers, he had collected a European Cup Winners' Cup medal after the team's triumph in Barcelona. The following year in the Scottish Cup, McLean's 'double' against Hibernian at Easter Road (in a replay) sent the Ibrox men through to the quarter-final. They would soon face old friends Celtic in the famous Centenary Final of 1973 and lift the old trophy on a 3-2 scoreline.

In the winger's first championship season at the club (1974/75), he was joint second top scorer with Derek Johnstone on fourteen goals. Only striker Derek Parlane surpassed that with a total of seventeen strikes. Celebrations were even heartier twelve months down the line, when a domestic 'treble' was in the bag. Two years later, the feat was repeated and Jock Wallace was in the history books as the first Rangers manager to guide the club to two such milestones.

McLean's last trophies with Rangers were both cups, Scottish and League, in Season 1978/79. Following defeat by Aberdeen in the Scottish Cup Final of May 1983, the player retired and became assistant to manager John Greig at Ibrox. He then worked with Jock Wallace (during his second spell in charge of the 'Light Blues') before going on to manage Morton, Motherwell (and a Scottish Cup win in 1991), Hearts and Dundee United. Tommy McLean returned to his spiritual home in the summer of 2001 to fill the new position of 'Director of Youth Development' at the club's Auchenhowie training complex on the outskirts of Glasgow.

Any player would be honoured to stand comparison with the likes of Waddell, Scott and Henderson. Indeed, in the opinion of many 'follow-followers', Tommy McLean actually topped the list.

TOMMY McLEAN

JORG ALBERTZ

On that highly charged May day in 1999, when Rangers famously secured the League Championship in the Parkhead cauldron, it was the coolest man on the park who stepped forward to convert the most important penalty of the year and give his side a crucial two goal advantage just before half-time. The iceman Jorg Albertz had once again delivered a hammer blow to Celtic. Manager Walter Smith brought the German midfielder to Ibrox from Bundesliga outfit Hamburg (where he was club captain) for Season 1996/97. In that first year, Jorg scored in five consecutive victories - against Hearts at Tynecastle in December (4-1), Raith Rovers and Celtic at 'home' (4-0 and 3-1 respectively), Hibernian (2-1, Easter Road) and the 4-0 Glasgow drubbing of Aberdeen in January 1997. Now firmly established as one of the fans' favourites, Albertz had more than made his mark on the road to 'Nine in a Row'.

HEART

His goal in the aforementioned 3-1 'Ne'erday' clash with Celtic is rightly considered to be one of the greatest strikes ever seen at Ibrox. Both the five-man defensive wall and 'keeper Kerr could only watch in astonishment as this 'Jorg Special' (a free-kick from some thirty yards) clocked a maximum speed of 79.8 miles per hour on route to glory at the Broomloan Road end of the ground.

Despite the fact that the player had his critics the next season, his overall contribution to the team was still vital. Several important goals included the late, late winner in the capital when his twenty-five yard effort in the 87th minute arced over Hibs 'keeper Bryan Gunn and dipped into the net to secure a 2-1 victory. But probably the midfielder's best that year were once again saved for old rivals Celtic in April. With only two minutes remaining in the Scottish Cup semi-final encounter, Jorg scored a stunning solo effort which finally ended all those green dreams of a possible domestic 'treble' (2-1, 5.4.98). Then, one week later, another similar individual strike in the 2-0 Ibrox league victory gave Rangers more than just a little hope in the final stages of that year's league race.

JORG ALBERTZ

SOUL

albertz

With the arrival of Dick Advocaat for Season 1998/99, there were changes aplenty on (and off) the park but Albertz continued to endear himself to the Rangers faithful. In August, the midfielder scored in three successive league matches when Motherwell (2-1, 15.8.98), Kilmarnock (3-1, 22.8.98) and St. Johnstone (4-0, 29.8.98) were the opponents. Then, in addition to his winner in the League Cup Final with St. Johnstone (2-1, 29.11.98) and an impressive 'hat-trick' against Dundee in February (his first in senior football and the first by any Rangers player that year), it was another of his amazing strikes which almost took the 'Light Blues' past Parma in the UEFA Cup tie in Italy. By season's end, his total was nineteen in all competitions. Not bad for a midfielder!

The following year, when the team arrived at McDiarmid Park in April to secure two in a row, his tally of 14 league goals at that stage (which included a famous 'double' when Celtic were thumped 4-0 in late March) was only two short of the figure achieved by top-scorer Rod Wallace for the same period.

Injuries seemed to haunt both player and club throughout the dreadful season that was 2000/01 but his 'Player of the Month' award for May (as the league campaign drew to a close) was richly deserved after a series of superb individual displays and goals against Hearts, Kilmarnock and Hibernian. After a lap of honour at the end of the final Ibrox league game (with Hibs), the hammer blow came with the confirmation that he was indeed leaving Rangers and returning to Germany to play for his old club Hamburg. The adopted son was going home to complete the circle started back in 1996.

Someone once commented that one of the main reasons the midfielder was held in such high esteem down Govan way was because the player never felt he was better than any supporter. In many ways, he was simply a brother to the Ibrox legions and, for this reason alone, Jorg Albertz will always be remembered as a true Ranger.

JORG ALBERTZ

OLD FIRM QUIZ

1. Name the scorers when Celtic were demolished 5-1 at Ibrox in November 2000.

2. Which Celtic player was sent off during the above game?

3. Name the Englishman who made his 'Old Firm' debut in August 1988 and scored in the same match.

4. What was the final result that day?

5. Jorg Albertz netted twice when Rangers won the Championship at Celtic Park in May 1999. True or false?

6. Can you name the defender who took the place of Chris Woods in goal after the Englishman had been sent off in the 'Old Firm' clash of October 1987?

7. Rangers have scored five goals at Celtic Park. True or false?

8. The Scottish Cup Final of 1966 required a replay after a goalless first match. Name the Dane who scored the legendary winner four days later.

9. What was the connection between the 'Ne'erday' game of January 1975 and that season's championship race?

10. Who scored the only goal of the game in the 1999 Scottish Cup Final against Celtic?

Answers on page 64.

MICHAEL MOLS

31

KENNY MILLER

Way back in October 1974 during the Jock Wallace era, a famous Ibrox striker hit five goals 'away' to Dunfermline when the Fife side were crushed 6-1 in the league. Although Italian Marco Negri netted a similar total when Dundee United visited Govan in 1997, it would be twenty-five years before any Scottish-born player wearing the blue of Rangers would equal this stunning scoring feat of Derek Parlane. Fast forward to November 4, 2000, and the league encounter with St. Mirren at Ibrox – a day that Kenny Miller would certainly consider to be more than just a 'wee' bit special.

A £2 million summer signing from Hibernian, the young hit-man (and one for the future) scored in his first game for the 'Light Blues' after taking to the field as substitute in the game with Kilmarnock (4-2, 5.8.2000). Then, just over two months later, he made the starting line-up for the first time and proceeded to claim another in the 2-1 'away' victory with St. Johnstone in Perth. Following his strike in the CIS Cup clash with Dundee United at Ibrox (2-0, 31.10.2000), a rich vein of form resulted in seven goals in three successive outings, the first of which was that amazing match with St. Mirren in early November.

Although Rangers were overwhelming 7-1 victors that Saturday afternoon, all the following day's headlines rightly belonged to young Kenneth who, barely midway through the first period, had already netted three times. His first (in just two minutes) came after 'keeper Scrimgour had fisted away a de Boer corner, the second (twenty-one minutes later) following a back post ball from Arthur Numan and the third (his 'hat-trick') was a direct header from a supremely accurate Albertz cross. Just for good measure, it was his favoured right foot again for goal number four after lead-up work by captain Barry Ferguson in thirty-two minutes. Shell shocked Paisley 'Buddies' no doubt welcomed the half-time whistle with some relief but, unfortunately for them, the second period was much of the same!

Sandwiched between strikes from both Billy Dodds (57 mins) and Neil McCann (90 mins), Miller's fifth of the day was a rasping twenty-five yard shot which left the 'keeper with no chance. He might even have claimed a sixth two minutes before the end but Scrimgour tipped his powerful drive over the bar. Nevertheless, the young man had done his work and was now ready to join fellow Scot Derek Parlane (and the record created some five years before Miller's actual birth) in the Rangers history books.

Despite claiming the opener three days later in his Champions' League debut, Rangers failed to progress into the second phase of the competition. The resultant 2-2 Ibrox draw, with French outfit Monaco, had not been enough for the team to gain a place amongst the elite of Europe. Back on domestic duty the following Sunday, however, the youngster scored again when Aberdeen were beaten 2-1in the granite city and three precious league points returned to Glasgow.

Even although the campaign had not yet reached the halfway stage, no other Rangers player would 'do a Kenny' and score in four successive games that season. As for the 'high five' achieved against St. Mirren, few fans expect that unique feat to be emulated for quite some considerable time.

And who knows, one day, it may even be by Miller himself!

KENNY MILLER

THE MANAGERS

WILLIAM WILTON, 1899-1920

(Match Secretary 18891-1899)

League Champions: 1891, 1899, 1900, 1901, 1902, 1911, 1912, 1913, 1918, 1920.

Scottish Cup Winners: 1894, 1897, 1898, 1903.

WILLIAM STRUTH, 1920-1954

League Champions: 1921, 1923, 1924, 1925, 1927, 1928, 1929, 1930, 1931, 1933, 1934, 1935, 1937, 1939, 1947, 1949, 1950, 1953.

Scottish Cup Winners: 1928, 1930, 1932, 1934, 1935, 1936, 1948, 1949, 1950, 1953.

League Cup Winners: 1946/47 (first-ever competition), 1948/49.

SCOT SYMON, 1954-1967

League Champions: 1956, 1957, 1959, 1961, 1963, 1964.

Scottish Cup Winners: 1960, 1962, 1963, 1964, 1966.

League Cup Winners: 1960/61, 1961/62, 1963/64, 1964/65.

European Cup Winners' Cup: Runners-Up 1961, 1967.

DAVID WHITE, 1967-1969

Manager David White came so close to championship glory in Season 1967/68. With just three games remaining, Rangers were one point ahead of Celtic but a 3-3 draw with Morton enabled the Parkhead side to draw level. It was all down to the last league game but Rangers were beaten (for the first time in that season's championship race) when Aberdeen won 3-2 at Ibrox. By winning their own game, Celtic lifted the title by two points.

WILLIE WADDELL, 1969-1972

League Cup Winners: 1970/71

European Cup Winners' Cup: 1972.

JOCK WALLACE, 1972-1978 and 1983-1986

League Champions: 1975, 1976, 1978.

Scottish Cup Winners: 1973, 1976, 1978.

League Cup Winners: 1975/76, 1977/78, 1983/84, 1984/85.

JOHN GREIG, 1978-1983
Scottish Cup Winners: 1979, 1981.
League Cup Winners: 1978/79, 1981/82.

GRAEME SOUNESS, 1986-1991
League Champions: 1987, 1989, 1990.
League Cup Winners: 1986/87, 1987/88, 1988/89, 1990/91.

WALTER SMITH, 1991-1998
League Champions: 1991, 1992, 1993, 1994, 1995, 1996, 1997.
Scottish Cup Winners: 1992, 1993, 1996.
League Cup Winners: 1992/93, 1993/94, 1996/97.

DICK ADVOCAAT, 1998-
League Champions: 1999, 2000.
Scottish Cup Winners: 1999, 2000.

GRAEME SOUNESS

RANGERS IN THE SCOTTISH CUP
QUIZ QUIZ QUIZ

1. In 1996 against Hearts, he scored the first 'hat-trick' in a Scottish Cup Final since 1972. Name the striker.

2. A British record crowd watched the semi-final with Hibernian in 1948. What was the approximate attendance?

3. What was unique about Season 1929/30 when Rangers beat Partick Thistle 2-1 in the Scottish Cup Final?

4. What part did Davie Cooper and striker John McDonald play in the 1981 final with Dundee United?

5. Opponents Motherwell were 2-0 up with twenty minutes to go in the semi-final of 1976. What was the final score?

6. Celtic were beaten 4-0 when Rangers lifted the trophy in Season 1927/28, for the first time in how many years?

7. In the final of 1898, Rangers beat Kilmarnock 2-0 with R. Hamilton one of the scorers. How did the player fill his morning that day?

8. Striker Ralph Brand entered the record books in 1964. Why?

9. Name the defender sent off when Celtic were beaten 1-0 in the semi-final of 1992.

10. What did most of the players have in common when Rangers and Kilmarnock lined up for the final of 1898?

Answers on page 64.

CLAUDIO REYNA

LORENZO AMORUSO

REMEMBER, REMEMBER THERE WERE FIVE IN NOVEMBER!

Premier League, 26 November 2000

RANGERS 5 CELTIC 1

Ferguson (34mins)

Flo (60mins), de Boer (68mins)

Amoruso (76mins), Mols (85mins)

Without a doubt, the season had been going badly for Rangers. Having dropped another two points at Dunfermline the week before, the 'Light Blues' were now a massive fifteen points behind their greatest rivals before this second 'Old Firm' derby of the campaign. Celtic, unbeaten in the league, seemed to be cruising towards the title and, prior to kick-off, were surely convinced that another three points would soon be returning to the east end of Glasgow. Champions Rangers, however, had other ideas . . . and that runaway green express was just about to leave the rails!

The 'Gers started with all guns blazing and should have been two up in the first three minutes but both £12 million man Flo and de Boer missed good chances, making the fans wait a little longer for the crucial opener. It was all Rangers and, in thirty-four minutes following Reyna's pass, captain Barry Ferguson weaved his way into the box before coolly slotting past Douglas. Although Boyd nearly buried a Jorg Albertz cross into his own net, the interval score remained at just one nil despite blue being the only colour on view that first-half.

Early in the second period, somewhat surprisingly considering the events of those first forty-five minutes, the visitors equalised through Larsson. Their euphoria was short-lived, however, as the 'Light Blue' lead was restored almost immediately courtesy of debutant Tore Andre Flo - from a de Boer corner, the big Norwegian flicked the ball home from close range after an Albertz header had rebounded off the bar. Then it was number three as creator became destroyer when de Boer himself scored for the first time in two months, heading home at the back post from a superbly judged Albertz corner. By this time, Celtic had lost midfielder Thompson (red-carded after two bookable offences) and, with rampant Rangers now in absolute control, it was simply a case of how many the Ibrox outfit would score before the curtain fell.

Next to take a bow was Lorenzo Amoruso, whose powerful, penalty box header (from another Albertz corner) left 'keeper Douglas well beaten before substitute Michael Mols (having replaced Kenny Miller) finalised matters with number five, guiding home after good build-up work from both de Boer and Albertz. The rout was complete and, although that was an end to the goals, the singing (along with several renditions of that catchy little ditty 'We Can See You Sneaking Out') carried on just a little longer!

If nothing else, the game proved once and for all that Dick Advocaat's side, with a full squad of fit players, was more than a match for anyone. Certainly November's other famous son, Guy Fawkes, would have been hugely impressed by the rather special brand of Rangers fireworks on show that afternoon, even although they missed his anniversary by three weeks!

Rangers : Klos, Konterman, Wilson, Amoruso, Reyna, de Boer, Ferguson, Albertz, Numan, Miller and Flo.

RANGERS
AND THE LEAGUE
CHAMPIONSHIP
Q U I Z

1. Who scored for Rangers when the Championship was finally secured at Perth in April 2000?

2. How many points separated Celtic and the champions that year?

3. Rangers' '9-IN-A-ROW' began and ended in which seasons?

4. His 'double' against Aberdeen in the last game of Season 1990/91 is the stuff of legend. Name the striker.

5. In the days before substitutes, full-back Bobby Shearer famously played in goal when 'keeper Billy Ritchie was injured during a Hearts game in October 1960. For how long?

6. How many times have the club won the Scottish League Championship?

7. Name the provincial club who finished second to Rangers in the race for the flag in Season 1994/95.

8. Whose goal at Pittodrie started the celebrations in May 1987?

9. In 1992, when Ally McCoist became the first Scot to win Europe's 'Golden Boot' award, how many league goals did he score?

10. Who netted five times when Queen of the South were thrashed 8-0 on the way to the Championship in 1956?

Answers on page 64.

LORENZO AMORUSO

DAYS OF THUNDER

A look back at Season 1992/93 when Walter Smith's side not only secured a domestic 'treble' (the club's fifth and the first clean sweep since 1978) but also came so, so close to European glory in the Champions' Cup. It was a glorious time when legends such as Goram, Gough, McCoist and Hateley wore the blue of Rangers.

THE EUROPEAN CHAMPIONS' CUP

It all began at Ibrox in mid September 1992 when Danish Champions Lyngby BK were beaten 2-0 with goals from Mark Hateley and Pieter Huistra. The return leg in Copenhagen, two weeks later, was no formality but Ian Durrant's solitary strike was enough to give Rangers a Scandinavian victory and the Blues Brothers' European Tour' was up and running. English Champions Leeds United were next on the agenda and, of course, the small matter of a 'Battle of Britain' encounter!

Certainly the first leg in Govan started badly (Gary McAllister had given the visitors an opening-minute lead) but the 'Light blues' rallied and, after much pressure, equalised when a very nervous 'keeper John Lukic punched the ball into his own net from an Ian Durrant corner. Ally McCoist then made it two (from another corner) and the stage was set for an intriguing Elland Road rematch. Despite being written off by the English press, Rangers' performance that night in Yorkshire was the stuff of legend. An early goal from Hateley (a vicious strike that arced and dipped behind Lukic) calmed any nerves before McCoist finally settled matters with a glorious second-half header from Hateley's pinpoint cross. Although the magnificent Andy Goram was eventually beaten near the end (by Cantona), the unbiased Leeds crowd, recognising a truly majestic team performance, gave the Ibrox outfit a standing ovation on the final whistle.

Rangers then joined Olympique Marseille, CSKA Moscow and Club Bruges in Group A and the league stage of the tournament. On a dreadfully wet and windy November night in Glasgow, Marseille were quite superb and led 2-0 before goals from substitute Gary McSwegan (with virtually his first touch) and 'Attila' (a brave, diving header late-on) salvaged a point. Few have forgotten the awesome sound that greeted Mark Hateley's equaliser – it nearly lifted the roof off the stadium!

Due to the severity of the Russian winter, the December 'away' encounter with CSKA Moscow was played in Germany, where Ian Ferguson's deflected strike (the only goal of the game) confirmed victory. It was early March before the lads travelled to Belgium, where they drew with Bruges, thanks to Huistra's second-half effort. When the teams met again in Glasgow, Rangers took the lead courtesy of Durrant. Hateley was sent off, Bruges equalised early in the second period and defender Scott Nisbet claimed the winner! The hostile atmosphere of the Velodrome (favourites Marseille's home ground) was the next port of call, with both teams realising a win would secure a final place. Although Rangers fell behind in the first period, they rallied in the second and Durrant's equaliser secured a 1-1 draw. Rangers had become the first visitors in 15 European ties to avoid defeat in this intimidating arena and it was now all down to the last game with CSKA Moscow. Despite creating numerous chances, Rangers failed to score and, with Marseille controversially winning in Belgium, their fate was sealed.

ALLY McCOIST

THE LEAGUE CHAMPIONSHIP

Title no. 43 was secured against Airdrie at Broomfield on 1 May, 1993 (when a solitary Gary McSwegan goal won the game), confirming Rangers' superiority in Scotland for the fifth year in succession. Second placed Aberdeen were still in with a remote chance when the teams clashed in Glasgow in late March but Rangers 2-0 victory that night answered any lingering questions. In truth, the Dons had been no real match for the champions and Rangers won the first three of their four league encounters. Although the team from the north triumphed in the last of that quartet (the penultimate game of the 1992/93 season), by that time the silverware was already on display in the Ibrox Trophy Room! Celtic finished in third spot, thirteen points behind the blue crew, on a total of 60. In the 'Old Firm' matches, Rangers won two (both by 1-0 scores), drew one and lost the other. The first of those essential victories came in the November Parkhead game, just three days after the trip to Leeds on European duty. Despite losing defenders John Brown and Richard Gough to injury during the ninety minutes, a solitary Durrant goal was enough to settle matters and take Rangers six points ahead of their greatest rivals.

Ally McCoist had netted an astonishing total of 49 goals in all competitions – 34 in the Premier League, eight in the League Cup, five in the Scottish Cup and, of course, those two most memorable strikes against Leeds in the European Cup. For good measure, 'Super' also won Europe's 'Golden Boot' for the second year running. In addition to those remarkable scoring feats, his front-line partner Mark Hateley claimed a very respectable 29 goals during the season.

At the back, goalkeeper Andy Goram was truly immense and duly collected both the Scottish Sportswriters and the Scottish Players' Union 'Player of the Year' prizes. He was unbeaten in 17 of his 34 league outings. With a total of 39 appearances each in all competitions, defenders John Brown and David Robertson topped that particular chart.

THE LEAGUE CUP

The first leg of the domestic 'treble' was achieved with a 2-1 extra-time victory over Aberdeen in late October 1992. On the road to that year's showcase occasion, Rangers had beaten Dumbarton (5-0), Stranraer (5-0), Dundee United (3-2) and then St. Johnstone (3-1). Not only had Ally McCoist claimed a 'hat-trick' in the aforementioned semi-final, but he had also scored in every round of the competition so far, including an earlier threesome down the coast in Stranraer. Final opponents Aberdeen had taken the scalp of Celtic before lining up to face Rangers at this stage of the competition for the fourth time in just six years.

The 'Light Blues' started well but Stuart McCall's early goal (after a pass-back mistake) was eventually cancelled out by Duncan Shearer's 62nd minute equaliser, albeit against the run of play. With no more goals in the regulation period, the outcome was decided in extra-time by an own goal from Gary Smith, deflecting a David Robertson cross past his own 'keeper.

Rangers : Goram, McCall, Robertson, Gough, McPherson, Brown, Steven, Ferguson, McCoist, Hateley and Durrant.

ANDY GORAM

THE SCOTTISH CUP

The 1993 Scottish Cup Final (scheduled for Celtic Park due to the redevelopment of Hampden) was contested by the top two teams of that season, Rangers and Aberdeen. The Dons, having already lost in the final of the League Cup and tracked the Light Blues' championship trail to no avail, were determined to end the campaign by taking this remaining trophy back to Pittodrie. By contrast, the Govan team (through to the final for the second year in succession) were just one game away from an elusive 'treble'- the club's first since way back in 1978 and those last days of punk.

Rangers progression in the tournament had been relatively straight forward (Motherwell 2-0, Ayr United 2-0 and Arbroath 3-0) until the semi-final stage and the game with Hearts. One down with just twenty minutes remaining, it took late goals from Dave McPherson (a former 'Jambo') and Ally to clinch a hard-fought triumph and a May date in the east end of Glasgow.

Although on the receiving end to begin with, it was Rangers who drew first blood on Cup Final Day when Neil Murray, the youngest player on the park, scored in twenty-two minutes with a cross-cum-shot to the far post. Then, just before the break, the majestic Mark Hateley made it two - his peach of a strike from a tight angle leaving 'keeper Snelders with no hope. With some twelve minutes to go late in the second-half, Aberdeen's Richardson (via a wicked John Brown deflection) pulled one back but it was a case of too little, too late for the northerners and the Scottish Cup was retained for another year as the most magical of seasons came to an end.

Rangers : Goram, McCall, Robertson, Gough, McPherson, Brown, Murray, Ferguson, Durrant, Hateley and Huistra.

Walter Smith's Rangers team of that period possessed quite extraordinary, special qualities and will always be remembered as one of the great Ibrox sides in modern times. Of that, there can be no doubt.

MARK HATELEY

1st class

TORE ANDRE FLO

Any player making his debut in the white heat of a Rangers/Celtic encounter would naturally find it difficult but for Tore Andre Flo, the burden was surely even greater. Not only was he saddled with a 'most expensive signing ever' label (following his record-breaking £12 million transfer from Chelsea only three days earlier) but also his new side were struggling in the championship race, a massive fifteen points behind the Parkhead side and runaway league leaders. Hardly a stress-free introduction to Scottish Football but, with much of the world watching, all friends of Rangers obviously hoped that the young man would cope with the immense pressure of the derby game. At the end of the day, not only did he 'survive' the ninety minutes but, by scoring on his Rangers and 'Old Firm' debut, the Norwegian was also welcomed into the ranks of a rather exclusive band of blues brothers.

Listening to the noise being generated by the Ibrox legions prior to the November tussle, would no doubt have reaffirmed the importance of the occasion to the player. Despite missing a clear chance in the very first minute, his moment of glory came early in the second half, just after Larsson had equalised for the visitors. Watching an Albertz header rebound from the bar following de Boer's corner, the striker was first to react and his delightful ankle flick found the back of the net to restore Rangers' lead with sixty minutes on the stadium clock. Tore Andre Flo had arrived! In many ways it was the game's turning point and the 'Light Blues' would now turn the screw on their oldest rivals, producing an emphatic victory in the process. Several years earlier, the player had impressed Dick Advocaat when Brann Bergen had knocked PSV Eindhoven (the side the Dutchman managed at the time) out of the European Cup Winners' Cup. On a miserable, wet night in Norway, Flo had virtually destroyed the maestros of Holland on his own and a 2-1 victory saw his side unexpectedly through to the next round. It was obvious that a striker of his calibre was destined for greater things. In due course, he joined Chelsea in London (for £300,000) and then, swapping one shade of blue for another in November 2000, travelled north to sign a four-and-a-half year contract with Rangers and become Scotland's most expensive footballer.

Despite missing several games, the hitman still managed a very creditable total of thirteen goals in twenty-one appearances before the curtain fell in late May. In fact, it was even a case of 'doubles' on four separate occasions during this time - in the matches with St. Mirren (3-1, 2.1.01), Ross County (3-2, 18.2.01), Hearts (2-0, 3.3.01) and Kilmarnock (2-0, 11.4.01).

Make no mistake, Tore Andre Flo is a class act and defences everywhere will come to realise that class always wins through in the end.

TORE ANDRE FLO

STRENGTH & STEEL

CHRISTIAN NERLINGER

Only a select band of players are given the opportunity to display their talents in the exclusive Italian venues that comprise the Serie A league. Fewer still of that elite group would decline such a tempting offer to further their careers in the Scottish Premier Division. In the summer of 2001, Christian Nerlinger became one such footballer when he rejected the pasta of Fiorentina in favour of joining Rangers in Glasgow for £1.8 million.

The German arrived in Scotland with an impressive pedigree that included more than 200 appearances in the Bundesliga, one of Europe's strongest and most competitive leagues. Many of the Ibrox legions actually recalled the powerhouse performer from two years earlier, when he was part of the Borussia Dortmund team that knocked the 'Light Blues' out of the UEFA Cup in late 1999. You may remember that, with both sides winning their home ties by the same score of 2-0, it was decided in favour of the team from Germany following a penalty shoot-out. Indeed, Nerlinger is a seasoned European campaigner and, in his early days with former club Bayern (where he first met Jan Wouters), appeared for the Munich giants in UEFA Cup games with the likes of Norwich and Raith Rovers. Despite interest from Arsenal, the player then joined his home-town team Borussia Dortmund in 1998 after a certain Paul Lambert left that club in order to return home.

The possessor of a tremendous left-foot shot, the 28-year-old actually made his debut in the German national side at the same time as the former Ranger and legend Jorg Albertz. The only difference was that whilst he scored in the game, Jorg was actually substituted at half-time! The midfielder represented his country six times before serious knee and ankle injuries cut short his blossoming international career but, by February of 2001, he was back to full fitness.

Many 'follow-followers' have felt for some time that a harder, more physical presence was required in the midfield area of the park. He may not be made from Scottish girders but Christian Nerlinger, oozing both strength and steel of the German variety, fits the bill perfectly.

FOLLOWING IN THE FOOTSTEPS

BARRY FERGUSON

Captain of Rangers! Membership of that hallowed body is strictly limited and only for the chosen few. In the past, Rangers legends such as George Young, John Greig and Richard Gough were all issued with an invitation and offered the once in a lifetime chance of joining this unique and exclusive group. In their case, the rest, as they say, is history. When the 'Light Blues' lined-up against French Champions Monaco in early November 2000 for the crucial 'home' Champions' League encounter, Barry Ferguson was poised to follow in their illustrious footsteps. The extremely talented youngster (Scottish Football Writers' Association 'Player of the Year' for Season 1999/2000) had come of age and was about to join the ranks of that select band of brothers in blue. Quite simply, manager Dick Advocaat had confirmed the playmaker as his new captain of Glasgow Rangers Football Club.

Undoubtedly the midfielder's proudest moment last season, whilst wearing the armband, was in the second league game with Celtic when revenge was in the air after events at Parkhead three months earlier. After both Flo and de Boer had scorned early chances for the home side, it was Barry himself who settled everyone's nerves by claiming the crucial first goal that Sunday afternoon, in his first 'Old Firm' derby as captain. And what a beauty it was! Without breaking stride, he collected Claudio Reyna's pass and, weaving his way into the penalty area, moved away from Belgian defender Valgaeren to finish coolly past Douglas as the stadium clock confirmed thirty-four minutes played. The delight on his face was there for all to see as he ran to acknowledge the acclaim of the Ibrox legions in the Main Stand.

Ferguson, a product of the Ibrox youth system, netted another three times that year when Dundee United (2-0, 31.10.00), Motherwell (2-0, 10.12.00) and Ross County (3-2, 18.2.01) were opponents in both league and Scottish Cup ties.

Considering the fact that Celtic won the SPL Championship with some considerable ease last year, Season 2001/02 presents a mighty challenge to both Rangers and the club's young captain. The good times may or may not be just around the corner but the fact remains that, sooner or later, titles and trophies will return to Govan. Barry Ferguson, captain of Rangers, will make sure of that.

BARRY FERGUSON

MURRAY PARK ...
AND THE WAY
FORWARD

On 4 July 2001, chairman David Murray officially opened Rangers Training and Development Centre (now known as Murray Park) at Auchenhowie on the outskirts of Glasgow. Built at a cost of some £12 million over a twelve-month period, this stunning, state of the art football complex defies belief in many ways and is surely one of the most impressive to be unveiled anywhere in recent years, standing alone in Scotland and with few genuine rivals either in England or mainland Europe.

Covering an area of thirty-eight acres, the centre boasts a total of ten pitches (of which six are full size), with £150,000 worth of under-soil heating installed below the main one to ensure continuity all year round.

An amazing twenty-seven miles of hot water piping will ensure that snow and ice disappear as quickly as you can say winter weather! Interestingly, all the professional pitches are exact replicas of the Ibrox surface, with the obvious added bonus that the players will feel no difference underfoot, either at training or on match days in Govan. Bearing in mind the joys of a wet Scottish climate, a £1.2 million drainage system has also been fitted to cope with those occasional showers that come our way! Similar to the type used by Ajax in Holland, the indoor synthetic pitch has a surface 'feel' of real grass and is specially designed to minimise injuries with its cushion base. In size, it is one third that of a standard football field.

The centre's £150,000 gym, with its highly advanced apparatus, is so advanced that the word 'gym' seems totally inadequate! There is, for example, an isokinetic machine, enabling recovering players to exercise without fear of damaging any weak muscles on the comeback road to full fitness. Like all of the high-tech equipment, this is connected to the medical department's computer and enables the club doctor, Gert Goudswaard, to oversee the entire operation. Measuring six metres by three metres, the hydrotherapy pool, with its own currents, is no ordinary swimming pool and is another essential component, not only on the recovery trail but also for maintaining good health and developing strength as well. Naturally, Gert also works closely with the first-team chef to ensure that the food on offer has the right balance.

Manager Dick Advocaat has made sure that nothing has been left to chance and all friends of Rangers can be justifiably proud. The future is here and now ... and the way forward crystal clear.

CLAUDIO CANIGGIA

FLYING HIGH

Rangers fans have not forgotten a rather black Govan evening back in March 2001 when Dundee came calling on league duty and returned home to Tayside with three precious points after a convincing 2-0 victory. All were in reluctant agreement that Claudio Caniggia was quite exceptional that night, having delighted the travelling support with a display that virtually outshone the Ibrox floodlights!

Hardly surprising when you consider the pedigree of a player who has worn the light, light blue of Argentina some forty-eight times (netting sixteen times in the process) and excelled in both South America and Italy with the likes of River Plate, Verona, Atlanta and Roma. Eleven years ago, the player achieved almost legendary status in Argentina (where he is nicknamed 'The Bird') when his World Cup goal sent bitter rivals Brazil crashing out of the 'Italia 90' finals. For good measure, he also scored in the game with Italy, the host country, that summer.

It was certainly something of a coup for the Dundee club when the striker decided to come to Scotland and sign for them last season. In twenty-four matches, he scored eight times. Season 2001/02 obviously presents a new set of challenges to the thirty-four-year-old player (who will most probably be the up-front partner of Tore Andre Flo in attack) as Rangers attempt to regain the SPL championship crown as well as progress in Europe.

One thing is certain however – wearing the club colours will be a 'bird' that can really fly!

RUSSELL LATAPY

CALYPSO AND CLASS

Although many neutral football observers assumed that the player was bound for the east end of Glasgow and Celtic after leaving Hibernian, midfielder Russell Latapy decided that, for him, blue was the colour and Rangers the club. A slightly different shade of green was not on the agenda!

The thirty-three-year-old player is a local hero in the West Indies where he previously starred for Trinidad and Tobago before retiring from international football prior to the commencement of Season 2001/02. Incidentally, his final game at this level, was the 2-0 defeat by the USA who are, of course, captained by Ibrox team-mate Claudio Reyna.

During his time in Edinburgh, the 'Caribbean King' delighted the home support on a regular basis and went on to become a firm favourite of the Easter Road crowd. With an abundance of skill and trickery, he is the type of player who can not only create goal opportunities for others but also score (spectacularly) himself. This is a rare ability, indeed, in today's modern game.

Those who 'follow-follow' are in for a real treat this season. A little bit of calypso with a great deal of class!

NEIL McCANN

ALSO KNOWN AS...

1. 'The Glove' was what he called his supreme left-foot. Name the Rangers legend from the 1960s, sadly no longer with us.

2. He scored twice when the European Cup Winners' Cup was won in 1972 and 'Bud' was his name. Who was the flying winger?

3. Simply known as 'The Goalie' because he was the best in that position. The legend lives on. Who is he?

4. Some called him 'Attila' after the greatest of all Barbarian kings. He was certainly one of the most feared strikers in Scottish football. Name him.

5. Defender 'Meek' was captain of the club and pulled on the blue an astonishing 635 times. Name the 'Light Blue' legend.

6. 'Bomber' always played for the jersey and was rightly awarded a testimonial game in July 2001. His real name?

7. A modern miracle, this Dane was one of the most talented footballers ever seen at Ibrox. Who was the 'Prince of Players.'

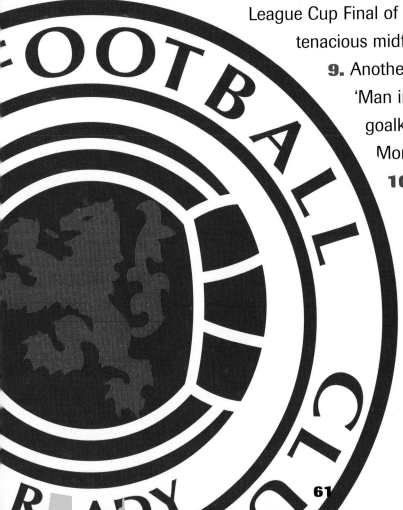

8. 'Doddie' scored the winner against Celtic in the League Cup Final of October 1975. Name the tenacious midfielder.

9. Another Scandinavian, the 'Man in Black' (and international goalkeeper) was signed from Morton in 1967. Who was he?

10. Dubbed 'The Crab' at Manchester United (because of his regular use of the square pass) before he became a Rangers great. Name the man.

Answers on page 64.

SEASON 2000/01 QUIZ

1. Who scored for Rangers in the opening league game against St. Johnstone at Ibrox in late July?

2. The defender's only goal of the season came in the 2-1 victory over Motherwell at Fir Park in March. Name, please.

3. How many goalkeepers were used throughout the various campaigns?

4. Why was early November a little special for Kenny Miller?

5. Who wore the no.22 jersey from late November onwards?

6. Name the new Ranger who could have been a Martin O'Neill signing.

7. Can you name the three players who each made ten European appearances?

8. Tugay scored in consecutive games during the season. True or false?

9. By the middle of March, he had taken his place on the substitute's bench more often than any other player. Name him.

10. Who gave 'Super Ally' his jersey after the game with Kilmarnock at Ibrox in May?

Answers on page 64.

CLAUDIO CANIGGIA

QUIZ ANSWERS

RANGERS IN EUROPE

1. 1961, 1967 and 1972. 2. True – against Sturm Graz at Ibrox and then 'away' to both Monaco and Galatasaray. 3. The German side were refused visas and the 'Ibrox' leg was actually played in Malmo, Sweden! 4. Mark Hateley and Ally McCoist. 5. True – in season 1978/79 with a 2-1 aggregate scoreline. 6. They won 7-2. 7. Bayern Munich. 8. 3-1 to Rangers. 9. Newcastle in the UEFA Cup, May 1969. 10. Colin Stein with five goals.

OLD FIRM

1. Ferguson, Flo, de Boer, Amoruso and Mols. 2. Alan Thompson. 3. Kevin Drinkell. 4. Rangers 5 Celtic 1. 5. False. Neil McCann scored a 'double' and Jorg netted once. 6. Graham Roberts. 7. True. 5-1, September 1960. 8. Kai Johansen. 9. Prior to the game (which was won 1-0 with Derek Johnstone goal), Celtic led by three points. Rangers would then remain unbeaten in the league and lift the title. 10. Rod Wallace.

RANGERS IN THE SCOTTISH CUP

1. Gordon Durie. 2. 143,570. 3. The club won every competition they were eligible to enter – a world record, since unequalled. 4. Neither played in the 0-0 first game. They were brought back for the replay and both scored (McDonald twice) in the 4-1 victory. 5. 3-2 to Rangers. 6. 25 years. 7. He sat an exam at Glasgow University! 8. Brand became the first player to score in three successive Scottish Cup Finals. 9. David Robertson. 10. 16 of the 22 came from Ayrshire!

RANGERS AND THE LEAGUE CHAMPIONSHIP

1. Billy Dodds scored both goals in the 2-0 win. 2. A massive 21 points! 3. 1988/89 and 1996/97. 4. Mark Hateley. 5. 82 minutes! 6. 49 times. 7. Motherwell. 8. Terry Butcher's. 9. 34 league goals. 10. South African Don Kitchenbrand.

ALSO KNOWN AS . . .

1. Jim Baxter. 2. Willie Johnston. 3. Andy Goram. 4. Mark Hateley. 5. Davie Meiklejohn. 6. John Brown. 7. Brian Laudrup. 8. Alex McDonald. 9. Eric Sorensen. 10. Ray Wilkins.

SEASON 2000/2001

1. Billy Dodds netted both in the 2-1 win. 2. Robert Malcolm. 3. Three – Klos, Brown and Christiansen. 4. He netted five times in the Ibrox league game with St. Mirren. 5. Tore Andre Flo. 6. Marcus Gayle was a transfer target when Martin O'Neill was manager of Leicester. 7. Amoruso, Klos and Konterman. 8. True – in the games with Aberdeen (1-0, 31.1.01) and Dunfermline (2-0, 3.2.01). 9. Billy Dodds, on sixteen separate occasions. 10. Jorg Albertz.

FIND THE LEGEND   ## FIND THE PLAYER